Cambridge Early Years

Communication and Language

for English as a Second Language

Learner's Book 2C

Claire Medwell

Contents

Note to parents and practitioners 3

Block 5: Growing 4

Block 6: Animals 17

Acknowledgements 32

Note to parents and practitioners

This Learner's Book provides activities to support the third term of ESL Communication and Language for Cambridge Early Years 2.

Activities can be used at school or at home. Children will need support from an adult. Additional guidance about activities can be found in the **For practitioners** boxes.

Stories are provided for children to enjoy looking at and listening to. Children are not expected to be able to read the stories themselves.

Children will encounter the following characters within this book. You could ask children to point to the characters when they see them on the pages, and say their names.

The Learner's Book activities support the Teaching Resource activities. The Teaching Resource provides step-by-step coverage of the Cambridge Early Years curriculum and guidance on how the Learner's Book activities develop the curriculum learning statements.

Hi, my name is Mia.

Find us on the front covers doing lots of fun activities.

Hi, my name is Gemi.

Hi, my name is Rafi.

Hi, my name is Kiho.

Block 5 Growing

Healthy Hana by Alex Eeles

This week we got a new class pet!
Not just a "normal" class pet, like a rabbit or a hamster or an insect.
But ...
a *ROBOT*!
His name is Buzz and everybody loves him.

BUT – there's also a lot he doesn't know. Our teacher, Mr Patel says we need to teach him. So, Teo helped Buzz learn to read.

Then Lil showed him how to tidy the classroom.

Going out to run around in the fresh air,
so we feel fit and happy.
Drinking lots of water,
so we stay clean and healthy on the inside.

I didn't know robots got so thirsty!

And my favourite one of all. Sleeping well at night, so we wake up full of energy …

and ready to do it all again tomorrow!

Let's be healthy!

Match and say.

Match each object to an activity.
Say what they are doing.

For practitioners

Ask children to identify the objects they can see. They draw lines to match each object to the corresponding action. Encourage children to make sentences using the pictures, e.g., *I wash my hands with soap*, *I eat bananas*, etc.

Buzz's dinner

Think and draw.

Think about and draw what Buzz eats for dinner.

For practitioners
Ask children to point to and identify the food items. Ask questions to check their understanding, e.g., point and ask *Is it a carrot?* Ask them to draw what they would like Buzz to eat for dinner on the plate. They can choose from the food items shown or other foods they can think of.

My healthy habits

Join the dots.

Join the dots to complete the pictures.

For practitioners

Ask children to identify each of the healthy habits, and discuss when or how often they should do each one. Invite children to join the dots and colour the items as they talk about their own healthy habits.

Story time!

Listen and join.

Listen to the story. Join the pictures in the right order to retell the story.

For practitioners
Point to the pictures and explain they are in the wrong order. Read the story and ask children to listen carefully. As they listen, they draw a pencil line to join the pictures in the correct order. Encourage children to use the joined pictures to retell the story.

Breakfast Time

It's time for breakfast.
I really want to eat.
The sun is up and I'm hungry,
I really want a treat!

I'm going to make a fruit bowl,
That will make me glad.
Full of my colourful favourites,
Which ones should I add?

First, I'll add some apples,
Some melon and strawberries too.
Then, grapes and orange and bananas,
There are so many to choose!

My fruit bowl is so tasty,
It's colourful and tasty and yummy.
A fruit bowl is my favourite,
It's so yummy in my tummy!

My fruit bowl

Look and circle.

Look at the foods. Circle the healthier ones.

For practitioners
Encourage children to answer questions about the foods they see in the picture.
Talk with children about foods that are healthy and less healthy. Encourage them to circle the healthier items. Prompt them to use simple words and phrases to describe the pictures.

Where does fruit grow?

Draw and say.

Draw the foods to show where they grow.

For practitioners

Ask children to describe the foods in the pictures, using simple words and colours. Ask where each one grows. Say the name of each fruit/vegetable and ask children to draw it in the correct space in the garden.

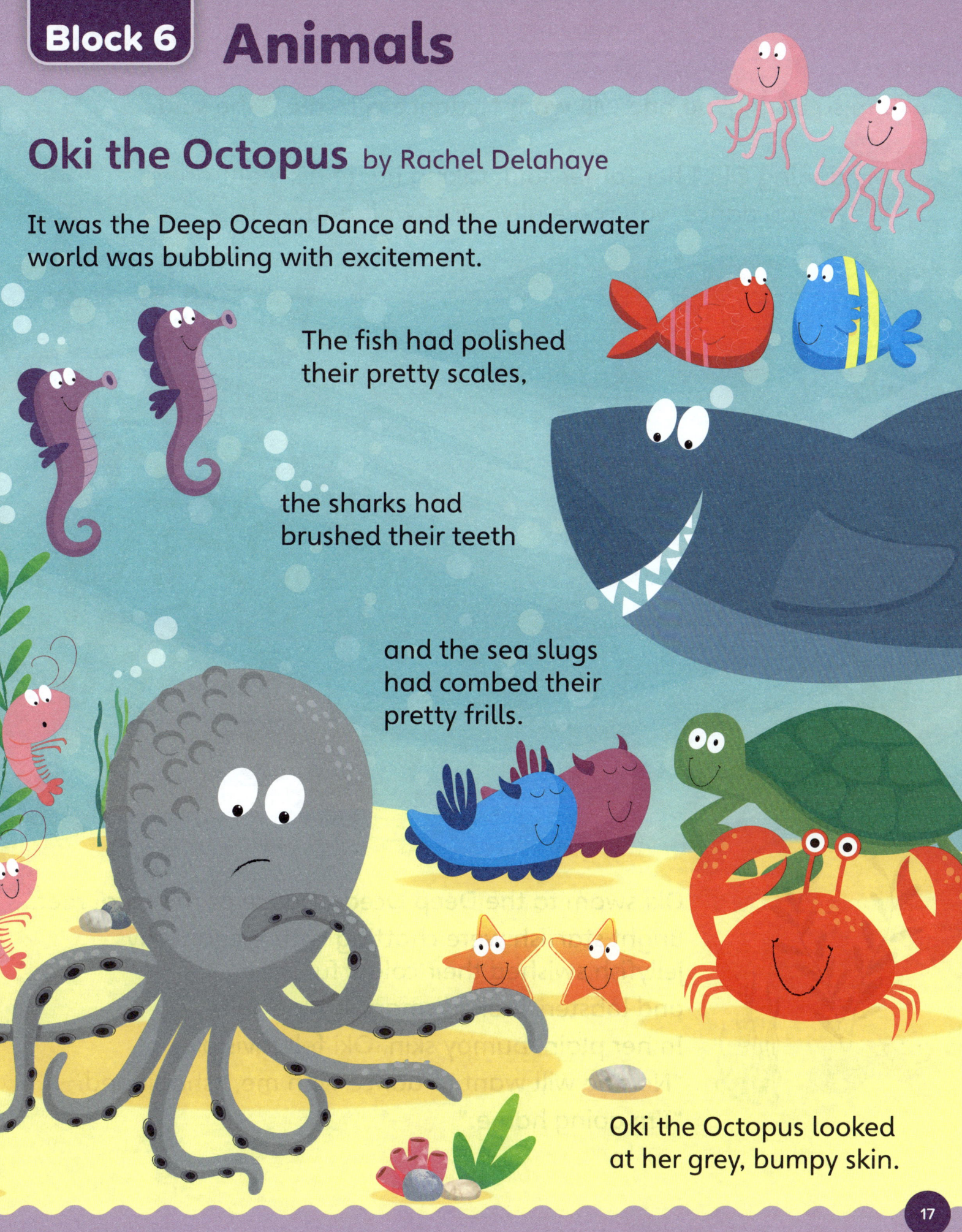

Block 6 Animals

Oki the Octopus by Rachel Delahaye

It was the Deep Ocean Dance and the underwater world was bubbling with excitement.

The fish had polished their pretty scales,

the sharks had brushed their teeth

and the sea slugs had combed their pretty frills.

Oki the Octopus looked at her grey, bumpy skin.

"I'm so boring, no one will want to dance with me," she said.

"My darling Oki," her father said, taking her in his eight arms. "When you dance, you come alive. Just wait and see!"

Oki swam to the Deep Ocean Dance at the coral reef. Bright starfish were chatting with elegant rays, jellyfish swished their colourful skirts and lobsters looked smart in blue suits. In her plain, bumpy skin, Oki felt invisible. "No one will want to dance with me," she sighed. "I'm going home."

As she was leaving, The Dolphin Band began to play.
They drummed on clam shells and blew seashell trumpets.
The music was so lively that Oki's arms began to sway.
Up and down. Side to side.
Moving to the music felt so wild and free.

"Look at Oki dance!" said a giant crab.

"Dance with me!" said a jellyfish.

"Spin me round!" a sea turtle said.

"And me!" said a seahorse.

"Me, too!" a sea slug begged.

Soon, Oki's eight arms were busy, spinning her new friends round and round.

And as she began to enjoy herself, her dull, bumpy skin did something amazing.

It began to change.

"Oki is turning pink!" said a giant crab. "Now blue!" said a jellyfish.
"And red!" a sea turtle said. "Turn green, turn green!" said a seahorse.

Her father was right. When Oki danced, she came alive! Like a fairground ride, she spun around and changed colours and patterns.

Oki wasn't boring. Oki was a star! And everyone wanted to dance with her.

"Turn red!"

"And orange stripes!"

"Lift me up!"

"With white spots!"

"Spin me!"

Oki was having lots of fun. She'd never been so popular!

But after a while, she wished that she was free to sway her arms to the music.

She wanted to feel wild and free. But how could she, when there were so many sea creatures waiting to dance with her?

She had an idea.

Now that she knew how, Oki changed the colours and patterns of her skin to look like the coral reef. And right before everyone's eyes … she disappeared!

"Where is Oki?" the stingray asked.

"Oki?" they all called.
"Oki, come back!"

"Has she gone home?" asked a little shrimp.

No, Oki was right there. She would appear again, but for a while she wanted to be on her own, to wave her arms to the music, and **dance, dance, dance**. Wild and free.

Can you see me?

Match and say.

Find the right home for each octopus.
Say the colours.

pink octopus

green octopus

grey octopus

yellow octopus

For practitioners

Ask children to match each octopus with the correct picture. Remind them how Oki changed colour to match her surroundings in the story. Encourage children to practise saying the colours.

Under the sea

Colour and say.

Colour and say the name of the animals that live in the sea.

For practitioners

Invite children to observe and identify each of the sea animals from their shapes and by revisiting the story. Mime the sea animals and their movements to convey and support meaning.

Oki likes dancing!

Tick ✓ **and say.**

Look at the pictures and tick the activities you like doing.

For practitioners

Ask children to observe and talk about the actions they can see in the pictures. They can tick the boxes next to the activities they like. Encourage children to talk about their preferences.

If You're a Lion and You Know It
(song to the tune of *If You're Happy and You Know It*)

If you're a lion and you know it,
Give a roar! *(roar)*
If you're a lion and you know it,
Give a roar!
If you're a lion and you know it,
And you really want to show it,
If you're a lion and you know it,
Give a roar!

If you're an elephant and you know it,
Flap your ears! *(hands at side of face, flapping like ears)*
If you're an elephant and you know it,
Flap your ears!
If you're an elephant and you know it,
And you really want to show it,
If you're an elephant and you know it,
Flap your ears!

If you're a monkey and you know it,
Jump up and down! *(jumping)*
If you're a monkey and you know it,
Jump up and down!
If you're a monkey and you know it,
And you really want to show it,
If you're a monkey and you know it,
Jump up and down!

If you're a crocodile and you know it,
Make a snap. *(arms stretched in front, 'snapping' together)*
If you're a crocodile and you know it,
Make a snap!
If you're a crocodile and you know it,
And you really want to show it,
If you're a crocodile and you know it,
Make a snap!

If you're a giraffe and you know it,
Stand up tall! *(stretch up high)*
If you're a giraffe and you know it,
Stand up tall!
If you're a giraffe and you know it,
And you really want to show it,
If you're a giraffe and you know it,
Stand up tall!

If you're a snake and you know it,
Give a hiss! *(hissing sound)*
If you're a snake and you know it,
Give a hiss!
If you're a snake and you know it,
And you really want to show it,
If you're a snake and you know it,
Give a hiss!

Animal time!

Say and trace.

Say the names of the animals. Trace their names.

I have a big trunk.

I am an elephant.

I have a long neck.

I am a giraffe.

I have big teeth.

I am a lion.

I have long arms.

I am a monkey.

For practitioners
Ask children to identify the animals they can see in each picture and then trace the animal name. Encourage children to say the sentences. Play the song again and ask them to mime the movements animals make and repeat key words and sounds (*roar, flap ears, hiss,* etc.).

At the animal park

Listen and write.

Listen to the rhyme and write the missing animal names on the park signs.

For practitioners

Invite children to observe the scene and to identify the animals they can see. As the children listen to the song, they can write the name of each animal on the correct sign. Some children may need you to write the names so they can copy them.

Acknowledgements

The authors and publishers acknowledge the following sources of copyright material and are grateful for the permissions granted.
While every effort has been made, it has not always been possible to identify the sources of all the material used, or to trace all copyright holders.
If any omissions are brought to our notice, we will be happy to include the appropriate acknowledgements on reprinting.

Thanks to the following for permission to reproduce images:

p16 Rosemary Calvert/Getty Images, bergamont/Getty Images, Red Helga/Getty Images

Thanks to the following artists at Beehive Illustration:

Laura Arias, Lays Bittencourt, Tamara Joubert, Claire Philpott, Sarah Pitt, Jan Smith.

Cover characters by Becky Davies (The Bright Agency)